SECRET THIRD THING

DAN HOGAN

SECRET THIRD THING

DAN HOGAN

THIRD

BOOK 06

SERIES 5

CORDITE BOOKS

First printed in 2023
by Cordite Publishing Inc.

This book was written, edited, and published on the unceded lands of the Gadigal, Dharug, Awabakal, Worimi and Dja Dja Wurrung Peoples. We pay our respects to Elders past and present. Warmth and solidarity is extended to First Nations people everywhere. Always was, always will be Aboriginal land.

PO Box 58
Castlemaine 3450
Victoria, Australia
cordite.org.au | corditebooks.org.au

National Library of Australia
Cataloguing-in-Publication:

Hogan, Dan
Secret Third Thing
978-0-6489176-4-9 paperback
I. Title.
A821.3

Poetry set in Rabenau 10 / 15
Cover design by Zoë Sadokierski
Text design by Kent MacCarter and Zoë Sadokierski
Printed and bound by McPhersons in Maryborough, Victoria.

 Cordite Publishing Inc. thanks Eda Gunaydin and Dan Hogan for their input during the production of this book.

10 9 8 7 6 5 4 3 2 1

Yowza! Yowza! Yowza!

—Emcee, *They Shoot Horses, Don't They?*

CONTENTS

PREFACE

We had a black-and-white hand-me-down until mum won a colour television in a pub raffle. It was then, in the early 90s, when I was about five or six years old, that my dad, a striking factory worker soon to be made redundant, helped me read a picture book about an anthropomorphic red tractor. It was my first year of school. I asked him why bother learning the words when we have pictures. His response was something to the effect that if you can read and write you don't need pictures, or a colour television. It is my earliest memory of experiencing an impulse to write for a reader, spurred not by a need for expression but by a curiosity to untie the alchemy of language. My brain could not (and still cannot) get past the question that if language can conjure colour where there is no colour, what else can it do?

Gaston Bachelard writes in *The Poetics of Space*, 'Consciousness of being at peace in one's corner produces a sense of immobility, and this, in turn, radiates immobility.' Thinking about it now, dad was talking about how language can be a resource when you're cornered by the traps and trappings of labouring under capitalism. With a red tractor and colourless TV in mind, *Secret Third Thing* was written from corners about corners. If I was to attempt to frame the face of the work in the eye of the reader before they meet the work itself, face-to-face (Oh. Oh no), I would say these poems are an argot against the radiation of immobility emitted by capital, against the ways in which capitalist configurations elicit submission without an act of submission. If anything, how a red tractor gains consciousness of the great many strifes produced by being cornered, and how this, in turn, sheds something not useful or useless, but a secret third thing.

INTRODUCTION

What characterises Dan Hogan's poetry is the way that, each time we come close to fully apprehending the impending collapse of capitalism, we are waylaid by something more urgent and mundane: groceries, emails, calls to Centrelink, traffic jams on the way home from work. When the present is frantic, frenetic and demands our full attention, it becomes the only thing that is real. The tragedy with which we live, in Hogan's words, is that we resultantly have 'no time to grieve for lost futures'.

This line, as do others in this collection, recalls Mark Fisher, specifically his contention that late-stage capitalism had caused the cancellation of the future. Unable to imagine alternatives to the present, he and other Marxist critics like Frederic Jameson noted the tendency of this epoch's cultural products to be capable only of referencing themselves, with the future foreclosed, and attempts made to summon the past landing flatly as nostalgia and kitsch. Starting with its title, *Secret Third Thing* is a hyper-real comment on this hyper-real moment: it is suffused with internet culture, memes, self-referential quips we make to cope, reflections on the lives we live, now, largely online, inter-cut with tongue-in-cheek evocations of the Irish pastoral.

But the past, the present and the future are not secrets. Hogan knows 'not that the world is going to end, but that it has already ended.' They also know that our cultural outputs form part of the circuits of capital which they are designed to critique: the collection is haunted by these digital traces, of algorithms, sold data and optimised desire. This is another thing that Fisher wondered, whether our desire to push beyond capitalism is inevitably always co-opted by and absorbed into capitalism. But Hogan is not escaping into being what we might call extremely online. They are not posting jocular outrage kitsch like, 'Rude epoch. How very dare'. They plainly ask: 'You think this is funny?', and later answer their own question: 'Elsewhere, glops of jokes make their way into a status update. It is an annihilative transaction largely misunderstood.'

The task for this text, like others with Marxist sensibilities – like Elena Gomez's *Body of Work* and Astrid Lorange's *Labour and Other Poems* – is twofold. The first is to clear up the misunderstanding at the heart of this annihilative transaction, by raising class consciousness. As Fisher knew, as Hogan does, the petit bourgeoisie has ways to prevent the topic from coming up. But Hogan insists on breaching decorum, noting repeatedly how capital perseveres through class: our familial bonds, addictions, symptoms, genders. To be non-binary, as these poems show, is not to just be a secret third thing – as the joke goes, not a man and not a woman – but to, much more seriously, bring class consciousness to bear upon gender, to ensure that whatever else non-binary is, it cannot 'match the interests of capital'.

The second task for the Marxist poet is to summon onto the page transactions that are not annihilative. Our lives now are structured by the prospect of an ultimate annihilation: the trillionaire class versus the collapsing biosphere. Hogan writes: 'the world isn't big enough for the two'. Above anything else, then, this collection is a work of dialectical materialism. It not only insistently names class struggle, but also highlights its generative potential: the notion that the opposition of the two classes may not be (only) destructive, but lead to the creation of something else: a third, new thing.

—Eda Gunaydin

Very Eyes

I saw what you did. Kicking the purple heads
off agapanthus. Telling me to suck eggs
as if I couldn't hear. You're like a hundred
diagrams stacked in the middle of a room
with all the furniture pushed to the sides
ready for a wake. Personally, my arms
are sad rope. I don't have elbows in the
traditional sense although I am known to
make bends to lift grocery bags. But don't
hold it against me. I've always been nothing
but a clump of clothes and cognition. I need
to start lifting my feet higher when I walk. Five
more minutes until the centuries-long careers
expo! Don't laugh. This is serious. It is claimed[*Who?*]
the sky is where the bats go to do their levitations.
Strike me down, sure. But remember you're never
far from a statue. Light travelling at the speed of sound,
sit back and unwind, un-suck the shinpads from
your legs. I would. Fall asleep beneath a glittering
sheet of quinoa woven by spheres. This and everything
on this page is the discount code you enter at your
last checkout. Printer/scanner/storm clouds in the offing.
Indensifies should be a word. As in the thunderhead
rapidly gains density before our very eyes. The hole
in the massage table is where you find your face. I
would. Eyes trained on the linoleum when the technicians
clad in jumpsuits don welding masks and work various
McDonald's burgers into your back. Don't think
I don't know.

I'M SELLING A LARGE SUITCASE?

CHAPTER 1

I'm selling a large suitcase?

CHAPTER 2

The second best thing I ever had was walking to do.

CHAPTER 3

The suitcase is large and I'm the one selling it?

CHAPTER 4

Wings. The difference is in the wings. Beetles have hard, leathery wings and long, membranous hind wings that they hide. Bug wings are made of two dissimilar halves. Hard at one end, membranous at the other.

CHAPTER 5

Is it true I am selling a large suitcase?

CHAPTER 6

Suddenly, it's the Olympics.

CHAPTER 7

Suddenly, I can't explain how I came to be selling such a large suitcase.

CHAPTER 8

My confidante arrives on time at our secret meeting location behind the Big Bad Walnut Café and Patisserie.

CHAPTER 9

Confidante, I am selling a large suitcase. I implore you to tell no soul about my large suitcase.

CHAPTER 10

My confidante exits.

CHAPTER 11

I decide to kick up my heels and take the bus home.

CHAPTER 12

Everybody on the bus stares at the large suitcase I'm selling?

CHAPTER 13

When I disembark I thank the driver?

CHAPTER 14

Walking home, I make a psychic note to disclose my dishonesties to any one of my confidantes at the earliest opportunity for I was not truthful with the bus driver. My deceit went like so: while it is true I verbalised gratitude, unbeknownst to her, my tribute was, in fact, an encoded thank you. A fool's gold. Counterfeit. A betrayal like a small flightless bird to the face. The bus driver should never know what I was really thanking her for.

CHAPTER 15

Metamorphosis.

Bugs are defined by their incomplete metamorphosis with juveniles resembling small versions of adults. Beetles undergo complete metamorphosis, beginning life as a grub and pupating into a hard-shelled, sometimes iridescent adult.

CHAPTER 16

At home, many people are calling me on my phones which leads me to regret installing so many phones.

CHAPTER 17

When the cacophony of phones ceases and the strobing anxiety in my stomach returns to its natural state of being a low viscosity deck of cards, I decide to kick up my heels ... again.

Unbelievable Meme Afterlife

With the addition of moon and moonlight,
masked characters and added rain, filth
at midnight makes for a life of prizes. I'm
not a cyborg yet. Homering into the hedge
for reasons, who is the oldest millennial?
Thwacking ectypal notability and mutation,
people are proof nostalgia is a political tech-
nology. Accept all cookies? Don't mind if I
do. It's starting to look a lot like ~~Christmas~~
the merger from (͡• ͜ʖ ͡•) hell ♥ Before
breaking the fourth wall please prove you're
human. Select all squares containing unhappied
transactions. If none, click skip. You only need
logon to squabble mazelike with remembered
information (͡• ͜ʖ ͡•) Select all the shapes
you can while lidded beneath
a frozen lake format
and if none tickle your secret third thing
defrost   Enter all the words below
with a heartfelt flamethrower. Click verify once
there are
        none. Separate each word with a space. I'm
already
        not a robot.

Unless? (͡• ͜ʖ ͡•)

No Alarms

Give the brigalows time to impersonate metal. Fold the final reminders like bed sheets. Ignore the echoes. Are you revolted the right way? Mosquito into the tidiest corruptions. Zap. Soak the stains. Ear against the wall, diagnose water hammer. Put the email address here if you are sending a copy you do not want the other recipients to see. It's always home time somewhere but don't tell anyone. Come bearing data. Using techniques, never live it down. Somewhere a landlord is kissing another landlord. Please clap. Consider the executive sated. Boil the kettle. Pour the tea. Prayer for meteorites. Oblivion coldens quickly when there is no-one to take a photo. Steam tentacles stopping in the air. Nobody actually knows how to count to ten. Fake it 'til you make it. Quake-happy fault lines at the edge of the whole disgusting sky. Please clap. Not tired. Just playing with my eight-ball eyes. Misery during the work shirt donning process. Head hole problems before breakfast. A cursed nexus. Tfw it's Thursday all day. The best part of being stuck in traffic on your way home from work is being late to the work you have to do for work after work. Clouds standing sentinel with their rain bodies above Old Guildford. The sky is about to happen. Please clap. Would you say your depression has a purpose? The air might be air-conditioned but who is ringing the bell? Ignore the previous email. This meal needs a nap. Please remember me to your boss and payroll manager. Dead leaves on the bonnet. New window wipers work. Couldn't sleep because dreams were movies that kept rewinding. Running early for once. Do yourself a favour and don't. Please clap. Do X number of things for Y number of means. Portending the spectre of an ending, remember to send me your bank account details for dinner. Emit an electricity of unshakeable compliance until the dawn of a new contract. Slurp. Slurp. Locomotion and food and why. False mirror enabled. So on and so forth. What is the warmest document type? What is the opposite of a chandelier? Is it fern spores? Submission without the act of submission. Ten days sick leave. A multiplicity of forces with no discernible origin. The doctors will call this a way of being on medication. Reports are due. No time to grieve for lost futures. TGIF. Please clap.

Old Growth / High Definition

tiny lantana clots burning in jam jars light the way
through the scrub / dragging a television by its rubbery grey power cord,
screen down, leaf litter churns and parts, ripping the scab off top soil,
a damp cut in the forest floor doesn't appear in high definition
and will heal beneath the din of galahparty and breeze,
we push the heavy nonflatscreen television inside a hollow tree,
moths clink the flame jars / eddying low, the moon is where we most expect it,
there will never be an apocalypse, you say, thumbing a quartz vein
in a pebble, tucking the power cord in, there's already been one
and here's a tree who's seen thylacines and war, but never
billboard shadows chucked on streams of traffic, blocking
the sun this way, there will never be an apocalypse, you say,
we already had one and this is where we live now / in the city, a lever is pulled
and a crane's arm slaps the sky, lowers concrete blocks

into the ground, nearby the last tooth in an escalator
disappears into a food court floor / our backs hurt,
televisions are heavy business, you touch your shoulder with your ear,
your clicking bones sing out / I crack my fingers / we agree
we’re at once smooth and putrid / a new step emerges atop an escalatorcase
while moonshine silvers the bark of this hollow tree, which will grow
to accommodate the television / we shouldn’t be here, you say,
the hollow tree will grow through the television, vine and copper tendrils
entangled for ages, even after the surf stacks up and so-called ~~Tasmania~~ floods
or else it rise out of the sea and frisbee off into space, grazing the cheek of the moon
on its way out / here’s old growth that hasn’t seen electricity travelling
to places we’ll never go, voices hutted in the walls of planned obsolescence,
here’s old growth while we wait for the fire to unclot the lantana /
here’s a tree while we try to think of something cool to say / here’s a tree

Everything will be okay for your landlord

You are what you eat so if you see me munging
on a hypertrophied human arm in the wee hours
behind a sand dune, no you didn't. Excuse me
while I shimmy into something a little less knowable.
Speaking of which, close all your eyes. Flood your
mouth with saliva. Hold it. Allow your hand to fall across
an expensive bottle of sun cream. Listen for the city
laughing at its buildings.   Now,   be a darling

and spit. You are what you eat so I guess it's time I ate
myself?   Nom ... nom ... nom?
I want to tell you so many things but my teeth
fly out of my face at warp speed. Not enough hours
in the day, which is to say conduct a prayer ceremony for
Search Engine Optimisation by washing your horrid bathmat
and use it barefoot straight out of the dryer   so nice.
It's bin night so there's that to look forward to as well.

This message and everything on this page
is an ad. Go here to end. Stub your second biggest
toe on the corner of the post office. (Required.) Nobody
tells you the itch is hereditary, that the link is coming from
inside the biography. If you like this, you might also like
the headache from eating ice cream too fast. Sit back and
look at the word *going* and say it out loud in the style of *boing*.
Play the Theremin with a boneless puck
          of chicken.
You are what you eat so I guess it's time I ate an exhausted
whoopie cushion? Summon onomatopoeia? In this climate?
Sir, this is Wellbeing Wednesday. Let them eat pizza. Nom, nom,
nom, etc. I might be two-faced but I wear one snood. Why are we
always doing things? You know how you hurtle

birthdaytowardbirthday
umbilical turn numerical
I'm wondering if you might do that one more time
but with no feeling. Recall the erupted fog.
So very un-fog-like to erupt, isn't it? Why are we always
doing things that could be interpreted as symptoms? We are
almost never in a helicopter orbiting a multi-story casino or
rissole? What's with that? Shell fragments and slow sand
stuck in our ears. A few more payslips
and we can start applying for a new

place. You are what you eat so eat your friendversary? It is easier to imagine the end of capitalism than a dry bathmat so eat a dry bathmat? The trouble with nightmaring across a field is the desire to smooch your own fractures. The thought of a list. A trapped nerve indexed. Onlookers gasping in awe. Failed empty file. Cossid larvae pattering the linoleum like big rain. Coins dumped in the sink. Is this loud enough? Everything will be okay for your landlord. Disappoint the oldest person you know by texting them: *Sorry but I can't make it tonight. I'm a graphic designer.* The sky splitting up like parents. You have memories to look back on today (content unavailable right now). This message and everything on this page is bad. Hold me close and

lol. What in the unsanctified insularity brings you here? Anti-ageing agent? You can run but you can't Dow Jones. You are what you eat so eat the rich. haha.

See also: ha. You think this is funny?

This is a serious recipe for a hotdog made out of the same stuff as a black hole. I want to tell you the story of the ocean trench at the bottom of the deepest single use plastic bag. Today I have a caffeine headache in my ass. Tomorrow you will enter a room carrying nothing but crisp impermanence. How very dare you. I'll have you know days perish. Road tar softens. An empty cup suggests water. There's always a cloth getting dry somewhere. 3.4 billion financial years ago a blob in the sea was the first thing to react to light.

Thanks blob. You were cool.

They say you are what you eat so eat a billionaire in space?
In space no one can hear you in space. Can't remember anything else. Can't even remember what is like

eggs in the presence of hailstones.

Can't remember a single thing.

Can't shake the thought that when I smile
I'm manipulating muscles to expose a piece of my skull.

Aduantas

If dolphins could fly as good as they swim
we'd experience things like dolphin shadows
whenever we went to the ground to resolve
undone shoelaces. This absence, too, is
a shape they don't teach you at business school.
You ever kick it with a dolphin's shadow? The thing
emotes homologous to the first time you witnessed
your smartphone screen shatter. The thing emotes
homologous to the titillation aroused by editing the
Wikipedia page for 'ventriloquism'. In the darkness
I thought it was a corner but it was a sex joke about
two walls coming together. Getting closer I thought
cat or ghost, for sure. Strike me down. Shone my
phone and it was a bugle announcing the invention
of flavoured milk(!) I went to school with a kid who
lied to me about dolphins. Said exercise such as
running would cause my brain to release
dolphins. I was working my first job before
I realised he'd mistaken dolphins for endorphins.
Going to tell my grandchildren this was inconsolable
intrigue. Nondescript respite. Nature itself. Ego inquiry.
Selective abstraction. Unmanned nonsense. Sweet
menace. Misfired association. Cathexis. Honey.
Fuck honey. Honey is the reason I got my tooth
drilled out. I was one year old surviving on powdered
milk and honey. My tooth went black and the nerve died.
Going to tell my grandchildren honey is made the same
way as fancy wine. Like instead of stomping on barrels
of grapes, workers jump on piles of dead bees and all that is
left after an hour's labour is a puddle of honey. Fuck honey.
Workers drunk on bee sting venom jar up the mess
with speechless hands and no gloves.

Creepypasta

Good evening. Thank you for calling Services Australia Centrelink Debt Recovery line. There are currently no customer service officers on duty. To find the location of a Centrelink say, 'find an office' or, if you're calling about something else, say, 'something else'.

Restrictions are easing but capital is not.

Okay.

Say what you will as millions of financial
(light)years tiptoe on your blood like a
password. Why did you have to go and define
your mask? Many things are not unlike the neck
of an extinct nightshade and yet
the crashworthy cloud. Sickening pipeages.
Multi-laned figments of desire taken
in by algorithmic grin. Hello? Yes?
I'd like to report a misspelling.

Say
who is in your family.

Misdrawn platitudes like a nose blown on
an encouragement award.

You can do a lot
of things.

Elsewhere, glops of joke make their way
into a status update. It is an annihilative
transaction largely misunderstood. Featherless
depictions of early drearihood gloss over the plucking.

So, tell me in a few words,
what's the reason for your call?

The dinosaurs with their feathers
all plucked out due to society's expectations.
What is an origin story if not capital persevering?
An anxiety supplied by decrepit
(pay)slips in time. Indicate interest by burning
butter. Hello? Yes? Painkillers, instant coffee, 4kg
of rice dropping to the ground as you
dematerialise. The download link will expire
but if the customer logs in, a fresh link will be
generated. This, too, will expire. It's an
unending you're not against. No lake chock-a-block
with heartwater here. Adore to be hemmed
in purpling sap. Collapsible but not
collapsed. When you said snow keeps
showing up beneath the piano, I took this
to mean anything can be a puddle (as long as
you're underpaid and overworked enough).
Is it not enough to headbutt the afternoon like finance?

What's
the reason for your call?

Restrictions are easing but the productivity index is not.
Rude epoch. How very dare.
The much frowned upon wasp is always
a working-age citizen. Okay. Don't talk to your sky
like that. Not when it is swollen with birds
with feathers like crowbars.

Forward
slash, safety net.

You would do well to resist the urge
to be a bonbon.

Forward slash.

See to a gearchange.

Safety net.

Pull the handbrake while driving backwards
and call it a reverse doughnut. (Reverse doughie!)
Restrictions are easing but
capital's psychic weaponeerings are not.
Change the locks. Change the locks
while the dreggiest abscesses hog
the quo. The words of another cloudcuckoolander
announcing unprejudice fall to
the floor like an unsliced ham. (Ham? One
ham!) Every time. Change the locks.
Restrictions are easing but—

I think you said, 'something else'. Is that correct?

Restrictions are easing but capital—

Thank you for calling.
Goodbye.

Castle

don’t you remember the drought and
the dried-up moat? the unmoveable brumby stuck

knee-deep in the mud? they were probably going
for moss on the castle wall

you lost your phone somewhere on the moat-bed

we walked around the whole thing

the pelican carcass?
diminished bill draped over rockpile?
you calling your phone with my phone

are any bells ringing?

how_to_be_the_best_worker_in_the_world.ppt

[**Slide** 1] You will notice all the best workers
in the world purport to be fisherman[*citation needed*].
[**Slide** 2] *Back when I used to drink I used to die.*
[**Slide** 3] Not to be dramatic but flies come from
nowhere. We know this because [**Slide** 4] there is
a placeholder for a life-sized life. Meanwhile, you
are to the vectoralist what surrealism is to advertising.
Lunchbroken and broke and [**Slide** 5] stand still.
Watch what its tail does. [**Slide** 6] Dad was a
fisherman[*see: Unemployed, disambiguation*] and so was
his dad[*see: Homeless, disambiguation*]. [**Slide** 7] Two images.
Side by side. A hotdog made from the same stuff as
surveillance. A life-size Tech Deck. Brainstorm
on the butcher's paper. First thought is the best
thought! [**Slide** 8] Delete this. [**Slide** 9] Who would've
guessed the best worker in the world was a spinoff
series of injuries. [**Slide** 10] *Superexcellent pizza
party in the middle of Wellbeing Week* [**Slide** 11]
The workers' honeyful argot regorged and maimed by
those who wear collared shirts to *establish credibility*.
For example: [**Slide** 12] Doomed if you do [forward
slash] Doomed if you don't. Delete [**Slide** 13] this disbelief.

[**Slide** 14] Commission misery first, the morning second. Daily template for success. [**Slide** 15] Icebreaker activity: describe your ~~addiction~~weekend as a ~~class struggle~~team building exercise without bescumbering the perpetual. [**Slide** 16] *If I ever die, which I probably won't*[*citation needed*], *crowdsurf my coffin across the food court at Westfield.* [**Slide** 17] Clown emoji. [**Slide** 18] An escalator step disappears into the floor with you. [**Slide** 19] *So drunk at late night shopping right now Sent from my iPhone.* [Slide 20] This page is intentionally left blank. Lossless [Slide 21] compression. Every day is [**Slide** 22] Opposite Day if you're alienated enough. [**Slide** 23] One million dead meme formats. [**Slide** 24] What is a professional development opportunity if not unpaid labour persevering? For example: [**Slide** 25] The crocodile is an ancient creature. One million dollars! [**Slide** 26] A distant shipyard horn sounds across the town, which is to say [**Slide** 27] Cowboy emoji. [**Slide** 28] Note how you are nothing without a caffeine headache. [**Slide** 29] Using what you have learned in today's session, return to your teams and show them [**Slide** 30] how to delete   this

Non-binary as in

fugitive. Not as in the shadow cast
by the command of the sun (even celestial
bodies are hologramatic constructs projected
by our fitness payoffs) but more tfw presented
with a bad batch of placeholders. 3,400,000,000
years ago a blob in the ocean was the first
thing to up its game by extracting value from
electromagnetic radiation within the portion
of the electromagnetic spectrum. See: light.
Thanks, blob. You were perceived.

6

Not non-binary as in androgynous but a deliberate
pluralisation of holes. Remember: capture comes
quicker to the rabbit who prepares only one tunnel.
Non-binary as in always being on the run. Non-binary
as in clusterfuck666 [burning heart emoji]. For example:
a premeditated dilemma involving sundials and wires
and relocating explosions. Non-binary as in a rave
of wind chimes disrupted by a flock of flaming eight
balls. Try not to hate me while I commission
the utmost listlessness and look good while doing it.

6

My gender is the bird with feathers on the inside
and crowbars on the outside. Non-binary as in
non-cooperative. A collective layer providing protection.
Delay as resistance. Not non-binary as in gender
careers expo or the fulfilment of post-injury duties.
Strike that. Defang the incitement of decorous lethargy.
Non-binary as the day is long. My hand is finally an
antler, which is to say it is on my head. Nothing else.

6

I've always done non-binary this way: gently pecking
my fingertips before placing them on the door of the
microwave. Holy. Non-binarily speaking? I thought
you'd never ask. We age like fine wine. A fine wine
that ages so well it is considered to be *futuristic*
and *before its time* and *completely untethered*
from the maintenance of the reputation of
transactions. Suddenly, crowbar plumage
pries open the casing of typicities. Untraps
futures from suspended animation. Infographics
mouthed by an image of the sky but not the sky itself.
This is how you know gender is a fossil preserving
the stratified history of class struggles. You dig.

Not non-binary in relation to bourgeois conceptualisations
of woman and man and femme and masc but non-binary
as in my interior world doesn't match the interests
of capital. Non-binary as in how else would you suggest
one kiss the microwave exactly? Non-binary as in
3,400,000,000 years ago.

I'M STILL SELLING A LARGE SUITCASE?

CHAPTER 18

Suddenly, all my phones ring at once.

Hello, confidante P?

'Pentagonal bone plates.'

You gesture at controversy, confidante.

'Take the stegosaurus out of storage tonight. Also, meet me at The Muskeg. I have desires.'

CHAPTER 19

Unlike most gaming parlours, The Muskeg of Hidden Accounts allows patrons to sell a large suitcase?

CHAPTER 20

The enjoyable qualities of the walk to The Muskeg boil down to the path's distinct lack of hex. Suddenly, it's Christmas.

CHAPTER 21

Mouth apparatus. Bugs sport a piercing stylet designed for extraction (think sap or blood or nectar). Beetles? Mandibles for chewing, cutting and grasping.

CHAPTER 22

I sit down at The Muskeg and refuse to kick up my heels. Confidante P has left a note in the tray of a poker machine.

CHAPTER 23

One side of the note is a rushed (but nonetheless engorging) oil pastel portrait of me while on the reverse side it is written: 'are you selling a large suitcase ... or not?'

CHAPTER 24

The message shoots a shiver so electric down my spine that even the most plagued bystander would mistake it for a monorail.

CHAPTER 25

(I secretly thanked the bus driver for keeping her eyes on the road and not on the large suitcase I may or may not be selling?)

CHAPTER 26

It feels like late afternoon when I leave The Muskeg but it is not late afternoon. Instead, it is the kind of Christmas that follows the Olympics.

CHAPTER 27

These days I mostly consider monorails as crypts for last season's moral inventories and spectral annoyances. Truth is, I've always been flatulent with money.

CHAPTER 28

The walk to the storage place is plagued by disembodied chortles, 1,000 dissimilar halves, and an ALDI.

CHAPTER 29

It is sundown when I arrive. My mind turns – as it always does at sundown – to the Olympics, but I'm still selling a large suitcase?

We're processing your direct debit

That's you in bokeh, hands leaking over a rail. It's coldest in high definition, loudest in standard. Trumpet like a mop along linoleum before it's too late. Ice cream didn't do this. Ice cream never does anything. Stumble on the buff tree root lifting a segment of the pavement. (Count this collision as a reminder.) You know who wins in the end. And yet you point at nothing out the bus window and call it the summoning of wordless data. Sent from my iPhone. Deliberately blurred portals for eyes. It's happening again. The nature strip caked in hard rubbish. Heap after heap grafted on. Waking to the sound of a disembodied whisper. Why does this always happen despite already being in possession of a selection of the most essential things? Do you cover yourself in a blanket or counterpane? Personally, my watch has stopped. Back in my day trophies came from playing our parents in franchise films based on the complete tea. Step outside (eyes shut). Gather that for which you're known (flavoured milk?). Just think how good it will be when you get to the end (of your contract). Take each day as it comes (disgusting).

That's you in bokeh, eyelids thick as chunks of fish bait. Earphones dangling from your head. Wondering what future moment might see you say something like 'more like hurry up and wait' and laugh and laugh and how we laughed. Accidentally sustain a lifelong injury via eating popcorn in the darkest of subcellars. Wreck kin in service of the ruling class but know it only as an illness. Dig a hole for the wind chimes. Personally, I turn my back on any reflection contained within the glass shower doors. Moss grows on this painting. The frame is rotten. The hook is bent. Take that phlegm flag out of your mouth. Fling it into the sink and wash your hands. Reject modernity and embrace traditional meta-modernity. Jokes. Peel a mandarin, pocket the skin. Time to walk back to the car no matter how much our legs burn.

Contested Possessions

Thirty-two dollars says feel free
to grieve the dead, love the dead but
this love lacks social utility. Thirty-two dollars
says Brisbane, not Meanjin. Says seizure
and not White Supremacy. Out of gaol

and out of the mines. Off the piss.
Thirty-two dollars says being identified
is not an identity. Says the fisherman
who knows a fisherman who knows a fish.
Total amount paid includes GST. What is a death

certificate (A4) if not dislocations
rendered colonial condiment. Red jacket
potatoes blister, explode in the colonisers'
Gregorian stewpan. Chattering grease flavours
spit. Wettens cash. Thirty-two dollars says

your purchase will appear as 'Queensland
Govt 2' on your credit card statement.
Please do not reply to this email as it
has been automatically generated.
You may contact us at:

Foiseach

Cluain located a semi-edible loomer, crinkle-cut and dusted
in chicken salt, tangled in Foiseach's beard.

'I'll be taking that,' said the Grimmest Reaper.

'Pipe down before you ignite Foiseach,' said Cluain,
plunging her hand into Foiseach's beard. 'At least make
yourself useful.'

The Grimmest Reaper perched on Foiseach's belly,
picking a knot with his scythe.

'I found something,' whispered the Grimmest Reaper,
indicating a small hard object entombed in a husk
of matted follicles. 'I think it might be soft error
or a jewel.'

'Let me finish the disentangling,' said Cluain.
'That medieval lawn mower you carry around
is a liability.'

Foiseach's snoring gob funded saliva streams
and introduced phlegmbergs into the environment,
compromising disentanglement. As Cluain and the
Grimmest Reaper worked through the hours for hours

and hours and ours, the droolcourse surged and settled, congealing to form a layer of sap-like preserve.

'We should be wearing gloves,' said the Grimmest Reaper. 'I can't do this anymore. I give up. Whatever is in there is not worth it.'

'I'm over it as well. Besides, it's a school night and I have a history test tomorrow. We should get some sleep. It's heaps late,' said Cluain.

The kids grew tired and cold while, outside, the lawn grew taller; multi-story green blades hatted by dewdrops, their crowns thieved by midnight gusts, splattered against windows. With mum at work and darkness thickening in the hallway, the kids could not fathom the journey to their beds for sleep. The Grimmest Reaper was quick to doze off after tunnelling into a dormitory of knots. Cluain travelled to the beard's end. Spinning herself into a cocoon of hair and detritus, she closed her eyes and replayed her history notes in her head. *And when the lawn is shrivelled by the discontinuance of its maintenance, knives of grass worn out and blunt, the dead patch left behind is the shape of disintegration to come, the last thing remembered.*

Summary of a knock at the door

Answers knock at door

NEIGHBOUR: Greetings! My name is Aduantas
and I live next door.

ADUANTAS: My name, too, is Aduantas. And I
live next door, too ... to you.

*Small amount of forced toothy laughter from both
Aduantas and Aduantas*

NEIGHBOUR: I spoke to your landlord, and he said
I could paint over the Anarchy symbol that's spray painted
on the wall we share.

ADUANTAS: No worries, I'll just spray it back on later.

Again: short, stabby chortles, flashes of teeth
Fake laughter between Aduantas and Aduantas indensifies
Crescendo
Giggly sighs

NEIGHBOUR: Well, I best get painting.

ADUANTAS: No worries. I best get—

*A balloon the colour of snow camo catches their concern
as it blonks along the pavement outside their homes*

The Floor Is Fuel Load

Two dooms are
        same game, same threat of nostalgia
        the living room is alive like a zombie
        and another inescapable commoditything
        falls in the house
and the floor is lava

One doom is when lawns tongue side mirrors
        Toot toot vroom vroom! (derogatory)
        and no mower can cut water
        and no mower can cut death
and the floor is fuel load

Three dooms are when
    1. money doesn't grow on trees
        (2. but fuel load does) and yet you 3. reappear
tearful from all these locked up assets and
quote unquote leaves

Long Simpsons Intro

the Macbook is providing the only light in the room
there is a noticeable change in the room's brightness levels
when the word of the day screensaver comes on
the word is diaphanous
the point where two walls become a corner
I never knew this room had a ceiling fan
handles are weird
think about drawer handles versus door handles for instance
I guess water in a cup naturally reflects the ceiling
because the ocean reflects the sky
Aduantas says he doesn't swim in the ocean
because sharks shit and piss and sex in it
and sometimes humans do the same
Foiseach says he knew a guy
who rubbed one out under the sea
in a shark cage for $50
and suspects his semen is still out there somewhere
on account of the third law of thermodynamics :(

a bird bath could be really terrifying
if it's framed the right way
use one of your fingers to draw a house on my back
why are handles so weird?
when did sun dials go out of style?
can my nose work like a sun dial?
like if I go outside tomorrow I want you
to tell the time with my face
when I feel the hum of your external hard drive
through the mattress I don't need a pillow
are there any bird bath-centric movies?
what's a horror film with a bird bath in it?
are you asleep because I can't feel you
drawing houses on me?
craving popcorn right now but I better
wait til tomorrow
I put a loaf of bread in the freezer
two hours ago to suspend its animation
I plan to unsuspend two slices of bread
each day until it's all gone
peanut butter on reanimated bread heated into toast
these are the loaves of our lives
I'm curious to see what this year's crumbs look like
nothing can stop me turning the toaster
upside down in the morning

Cluain

Who's keen to go down to the old mill and feel
dread? It begins with a petition to rename the void
Voidy McVoidface and finishes with a deformation
of impetus. This I know: there are two hearts
and one is a thunderbolt of history and the other
is a stomach. Stay with me. I'll shout you a scratchie
at late night shopping. Anyone who says 'anyone
who says' needs a shard of flattened hubcap sharing
circular stain with cement plus shattered remains
of bird deterrent CD not far from here, milk,
printer/scanner/milk skin, bread, a naturally occurring
denim cat, rice, coin, water before it falls, obelisk, meat
patty, printer/scanner/meat patty, daymoon because coffin,
hark the herald angels snivel NO MOW, bin night eve,
printer/scanner/daymoon because coffin, data rot niceties,
a grief that only HR can procure, seamonkey hatchery,
dishcloth, printer/scanner/rapid trasher/fogmaker,
unprecedented times call for an unprecedented
accumulation of vitamin canisters, bunting, severe
columns of light, not at all, printer/scanner/membranous
goop backstroking in a think tank, I keep fish near me,
cooked fished, sphered up into spheres fish, at all times:
onions, don't forget the fish(!), every morning faceless
saints chop credit cards into the toilet, dish cursed oblongs,
printer/scanner/micromorts, the value of a statistical life,

submarines rising on your skin instead of goosebumps
is a symptom of government spending, when the late arvo
southerly hits try to survive by using survival gear, valves
and pipes, where the sun once collaborated with the meadow
in displays of well-received saturnalia, submarines now graze
and nuzzle in the tall grass, if I was a graphic designer I would
specialise in a submarine wearing a top hat in Corporate
Memphis, enough of that, printer/scanner/fall asleep beneath
a sheet of glittery quinoa woven by spheres, jokes,
I would never, printer/scanner/remember to hit like
and subscribe and click that stinky notification
bell, do you hear the screaming? the screaming
is attached for convenience, sure would be a shame
if someone were to, you know, consider the environment
before printing this email, it is a crime against
private property to rest, keep dehydrated but
no worries if not, //\ (͡°͡° ͜ʖ ͡°͡°) /\\, friendship
ended with Holden Halftime, now KFC Video Replay
is my best friend, adore your Vegemite or perish, there
is little left to be said that hasn't already been blistered,
burned to disc, jarred up, printer/scanner/enemy problems,
Jim Carrey's character diving into a satellite dish, printer/
scanner/slowly thinning organ, 400 corn chips behind
a car and one shoehorn, what you gonna do? Fire
me?

Mate, I was born fired.

A Life of Prizes

Be the counterfeit queen of the premeditated
argot you want to see in the world / Rupture
this / Rupture that / A circle
          possessed / Know the last thing by
how close it is to the first thing / Remove
all your clothes /
                    from the washing machine (sicko) /
Learn the alphabet / ABCDEFG while huffing
black mould / Feathers / make good toothpicks /
Anything can be a toothpick if you have a go / Cop
a mouthful / The best form of welfare is a
feather / Phonelight floods the holes / in
your body / Soundless and high-pitched blue / Hit the snooze
button / Ten more minutes / of blissful
nowhereness / At a time when the sky has been
slapped, home is a gimmick / Mow a little lawn /
make a little love / and one day posh snorkel /
Yowza / Yowza / Yowza / Collaborate with doom /
(Doomed if you do / Doomed if you don't) /
Commission the havoc of birds
                    with feathers like crowbars
                    to pry open new skies / Time? /
                    It stumbles / as you stick your leg
out the window of your luxury apartment / How
do you find something when you don't know what it is
called? / A crowbar bird circles overhead,
                    scheming / The trillionaire class
emerges / and the biosphere collapses /
This world isn't big enough for the two

of us / (The Amazon and Amazon) / Doomsurf's
up / Hang ten, you are / an interregnum of
competing vectors /
        The product and the link rot / A great variety /
Finally, you are a transactional plane, the everything
store every minute of every day, a vector possessed
by a new ruling class / Jimmie the locks /
                Wait for the image to take hold /
                Shouldn't be long now /
                Yowza / Yowza / Yowza
If you liked this / you might also like this headache
from licking ice cream too fast / 1,000,000,000,000
/ What of the muted sun inherited? / The hour
dispenses its smallest trifles to its buffest
minutes / Troubles accumulate / Bin night /
Thursday / Late night shopping / The night is but
a kitten / Meow / See also: meow / A collision in
cahoots / See the cars parked in scarce clumps /
but don't take my word for it / Check the oblong
allotments / White boxes painted on black
asphalt / Describe zero as both nothing and a
mouth / Envelopment / What is a car park if not
the reaper's shadow julienned myriad ways? / So on
and so the evening arranges its droplets on
the sky's Keep Cup / Sip, slowly / Hands free /
Portending the spectre of an ending, enter KFC
dressed as Ronald McDonald / Be the counterfeit
queen of the premeditated argot you want to see
in the KFC / and one day a life of prizes

Onceability

Scarecrow a mirrorball lowered from food court sky.
Conflicting salts and vinegars streak motley across
glass of phone. Swipe right like a mop along linoleum.
Proximity to the bugs' choral is optimised to rage
in the face of optimisation/*demolition by neglect*

The night is a line where memories are data packets
transmuted by the year that is a careerist vine left on
seen in the group chat mirage, endlessly animated
check summing and circuit switching/*waterbeforeitfalls.gif*

Tentacles of fog vortex pedestrian overpass, no
graceful silo curved smooth like an empty egg. Always
offer to perforate. Fund a brief fractal noise/*work
shirts drying on the line.* Grow your fingernails
long to strum the ribcage of debt. Lowered from
food court scarecrow, sky a mirrorball

Seaweed ribbons zap soft moat-bed, uninstall
illustrious atrophy, amplify non-linear progeny.
Is memory a line where data packets night?
Carried committed to real radical hours
for hours and ours/*totalising sabotages fluctuate at the centre*

Awoken by sound of nondescript conversation starter
and skyquake. Refactoring code smell entombing data
rot/*demolition by neglect.* Under fault conditions
severity is implied by a scarecrow mirrorball
lowered like a glass mop

Proximity to the choral neglect is along linoleum.
The optimisation of demolition is bugs
and shirts drying on your fingernails. Offer
to perforate, fund a brief egg fog, graceful
overpass, fractal smooth like an empty curve. Tentacled
pedestrians face optimisation/*proximity to morbid stakeholders*

Carried where selective night moat sabotages
ribbons. Amplify non-linear seaweed and uninstall
the line, packets of radical hours refactoring bit
rot under fault conditions and skyquake/*always noise and work*

Mirrorball conversation smell awoken
by lowered sound. Starter code is a nondescript
scare. Left by the *waterbeforeitfalls.gif*, the year is
an endlessly seen crow/*data implied by the severity of glass*

The ~~four~~eight horse~~men~~friends ...

1.
mia (reverse centaur)
walks backward
into a fire station
eats most of a curtain
and all of two moths
that got in the way

2.
foiseach (one-toed, hoofed)
bolts face first through
a pizza hut window (ouch)
dies from injuries
at the salad bar (sad)

3.
ash (extant subspecies of equus ferus)
tosses a frisbee from his mouth
(there is no remarkable sound)
the disc takes silence with it
caught in the jaws of angela

4.
angela (of the family equidae)
(fixing a midnight sandwich)
is imperceptible in the light-hungry kitchen
(she didn't even know you were home)
when you flick on the light

... of the ~~apocalypse~~new normal

5.
cluain (equine-related concept)
eats a wallet they found
on the dance floor (amusing)
you don't clock them chewing
on account of the deep house

6.
sylvie (equivalent of the human fingertip)
canoes into the centre of the internet
and begins the evacuation
by convincing a family of whales
to beach themselves

7.
aduantas (no foot, no horse)
licks both sides of a dvd
and reviews: one side is sweeter
but now I must disappear inside
the forest yelling about money

8.
evening (205 bones)
kicks a broken link (502 bad gateway)
into the side of a moving bus
and a passenger hisses
back with increasing urgency
and politeness: my tongue! it is
not unlike the fossil! of an unexploded
bonbon! remember this!
warmly!

I MIGHT HAVE SOLD A LARGE SUITCASE? WHAT?

CHAPTER 30

Suddenly, the doors to the storage place fling open like a fuckwit.

CHAPTER 31

It's been a long time, storage place.

CHAPTER 32

I stand before my storage unit, the roller door disappearing into the roof as my heart shimmies in the post-lockout law nightclub of my chest.

CHAPTER 33

Dust rearranges the atmosphere and settles like a recovering snow globe. A tiny plastic stegosaurus (who shan't be named) occupies the void.

CHAPTER 34

I cup the stegosaurus in my hands, bringing its curse to my mouth.

CHAPTER 35

The little plates come off easily between my teeth. They pop.

CHAPTER 36

Have you ever seen a stegosaurus without its plates? An instantly forgettable and utterly unromantic creature. I take one last look at the stegosaurus, running my gaze across the gnarled nodules where its plates once stood like a procession of weathervanes on the roof of a houseboat ... except for one thing: it's a houseboat of lies.

CHAPTER 37

Two of my phones ring at once. Hello, confidante F?

'[inaudible] was a houseboat of truth and now it's a houseboat of lies. You are a traitor of the highest order, and you're selling a large suitcase?'

Hello, confidante L?

'Wanker.'

At that moment, I make moves to destroy the two phones. I return home and prepare a fondue.

CHAPTER 38

I toss my phones into the fondue. Plop!

CHAPTER 39

I decide to kick up my heels and ride the bus again.

CHAPTER 40

On the bus, there is not nobody, and I'm selling a large suitcase?

CHAPTER 41

I sit exactly in the centre of the back seat and hug the large suitcase I am selling?

CHAPTER 42

We pass many shops, all of them selling various incarnations of proteins or pianos or self-care products for psychopomps.

CHAPTER 43

I disembark, but I do not say thank you.

CHAPTER 44

Suddenly, I am stricken by a malady so severe that one can only describe it as possibly selling a large suitcase.

CHAPTER 45

I struggle up the stairs to my apartment.

CHAPTER 46

A voice from above yells, *asshole freak!* and a fish is dropped down the stairwell in my direction. The cod grazes my face on its way down, leaving a long sequin scale jabbed in my temple like a promotional bookmark.

CHAPTER 47

Fondue lavas from under the front door of my apartment as I fossick for my keys.

CHAPTER 48

I left the fondue machines on and now my place is flooded with fondue. Surely, all my devices are compromised.

CHAPTER 49

Time is caramelising.

CHAPTER 50

I turn back down the stairs.

CHAPTER 51

'I walked on your suitcase, wanker!'

CHAPTER 52

Out on the street, I throw my large suitcase around. Give it a few kicks.

CHAPTER 53

The ground is a gland. It pumps hot mist and secretes a sugary dew in the same way I remember the eyes of many mercurial bedtime entities emerging from everybody's favourite spoiled pond as a child. You remember, too.

CHAPTER 54

The second best thing I ever had was walking to do.

CHAPTER 55

I sit on the large suitcase I am selling?

CHAPTER 56

A little-known flagbearer with a heart of bronze accosts me and enquires about the suitcase.

CHAPTER 57

'How large is it and how much does it cost?'

What you see is what you get, little-known flagbearer.

Blade of Grass, Meadow of Knives

Summer equals cicadascream plus other superimpositions
hung in the air like an idea of bunting but never the worsted
wool. I'm no mathematician but who is? Nobody in this poor
excuse for a nondescript prism hurtling birthdaytowardbirthday
toward your tenth coffee is free. A popout cake is a large prop
designed to resemble a cake in which a person emerges to the
surprise of outsiders. Innovation and jobs and growth have seen
a little seat inside. When the alarm went off this morning I wasn't
yet the genealogy of an image but who is? Who? Everybody inside
a popout cake has two wolves inside them. Both are domesticated.
One is a Chihuahua/Pomeranian cross. The other is red. Anyway,
there is no gimmick like home. I once knew a Pomeranian who,
despite the limits of their form, taught me 'bagel' is short for
'baby angel'. I digress. But also: when in Rome? When in
Rome stuff a pie full of doves and frogs and have them burst forth
for your guests. This is all to say grief is a detour. (When in
Rome!) I desire for this loss to manifest as something (anything)
handsome in writing but all I've got is this fixation on popout
cakes and the loudest cicadas are the ones who stayed
in the ground the longest. But don't take my word for it. Ear
to the ground until the lawn's urge has cut through to the other
side. Blade of grass? Meadow of knives! Find a verandah and wait.
See what I'm saying? When in the yard ask yourself: what fangs
out of the bracken with a head full of garden? The answer and
everything on this page is

How to leave work on time

after *Jackass*

Ibis encircle bin the same way they do skyscraper.
Coincidence? We know who wins in the end. Hi, I'm Johnny
Knoxville and this is how to leave work on time,
the poo emotion solar groover. I've stopped
sitting still, spectacular obelisks hunt my loves. I've stopped
sitting. In the centre of myself:

> bees. I wish. Time to pole vault
> over this sewerage farm
> or as I like to call it:
> naughty water. Hi, I'm Johnny Knoxville
> and this is the circumstellar habitable zone, it's me

on the treadmill of your semi-historical attitude with the rest
of the marching band, what's the number for 000? The answer
is Hi, I'm Johnny Knoxville and this is an email from (sub)
Human Resources, reveal your fully optimised desire lines
before C.O.B. (of corn, partially husked), it's me picking
Blu Tack off a door with a bootleg wad, hi. I'm Johnny Knoxville
and this amalgam you hold is product integration, both natural
and induced, seek the funnel and win, hi. What are you doing on
the PC? Do one thing every day that makes you a rodeo clown
at 3pm, follow topics like nobody is selling your data, share
memories based on your search history, hi. I'm Johnny Knoxville
and this is high octane Blu Tack, Blu Tack me to the centre of a
diagram of myself, track changes, pin the nipple on the chest
of Growth Domestic Product chomped by the baby alligator
of selective adversity, I am annotated by arrows, the Reserve
Bank of electrocuted perineums, divided casserole, hi. My stomach
has its own stomach, my insides become outside in a pop-up book
kind of way, 2D but also 3D, with a number at the bottom, and
everything, centred, my stomach is dating another stomach, hi.

I'm Johnny Knoxville and what is a word if not a drillbit for the kleptoparasite? Use text boxes, no fill nor outline, sparkling uncertainty, dearest stomach, it is I, the John following an account focused on something called food porn, hi. I'm John Knoxville and this is a distress

signal
Sent from my dog's pacemaker

Ibis encircle your misery index the same way they encircle your most-favoured acquisitions. Hi, I'm Johnny Knoxville and welcome to amazeballs budget repair, immaterial improvement, the dentata of hair combs, the question asked of the city laughing at its buildings and what's that smell? What ambulance can be called? Where is the petiole that comes from nowhere and retreats into the place between materials? Where? Can't stay late forever. Poach to please with microwave ease. Weld the soup. Pinch the whistle. Drown baton. Wipe the frame. Suck the fossil. Hi. I'm Johnny Knoxville and this is the imminent arrival of friends, release the bees into the limousine and lock the doors. We know who wins in the end.

Post-Credits Scene

Your face raised dollar signs for eyes. An open
smile and protruding tongue styled after a banknote. Should we

stay till the end? A sausage roll like the credits roll. Sorry
for torching Notre Dame, it just looked so sexy on fire. The flame
emoji is depicted as a flame, the kind produced when something is

on fire. You say it as if automatic doors act on instinct and not
programming. Walk in. Scrunch an eye. Any eye. Doesn't
matter. Observe the products. Refuse discounts. Drink various milks
in the centre of the bank. The meaning of the wilted flower emoji can

be interpreted as a flower. Depicted by operating systems as a red
rose bent towards the ground searching for water (vibe slain), a petal
shed. You explain honey fungus. Root rot. Repossessing faded blooms.
The wilted rose emoji is dying back. Emphasis on back. Death above
ground means roots continue life underground. Not to be confused

with thriving. Remain still and suck air-conditioned air into a big pink
lung. See how long you can hold it. Stand at the forefront of a new
head office with bloodshot dollar signs for eyes. Open smile.
Your tongue

a polymer banknote wet with aspiration. Want to stay
for the post-credits scene if there is one? I don't mind
but it's your shout at the drive-thru on the way home.

Condition Report_final_FINAL2_updated_FIANL (6)

I stick my leg out the window of my feral continuation.
Time to wingsuit off this fuck. A well-trod lineage. It is inevitable
the garbage rises. Disintegration defined by a glitchy nod
at decrepitude. Path to monstrosity? Yes please. Consider this
extra task part of your professional development. I believe
in an interventionist Santa. Mutation? I'll shout ya a scratchie.
Everybody needs a small piece of church at the right time. So
drunk at late shopping right now. Why do people always
profusely apologise but never profusely pole vault? I stick my leg
out the window of my luxury apartment and can't believe
the financial year is almost over. Said nobody ever. Who is

keen to go down to the old mill and feel dread? Who? I stick
my leg out the window and livestream the rain. The shoe is wet
but the foot is dry. So many things are like an old saying. You can
lead a horse to Ferris Bueller's funeral but you can't make it
drink the funeral juice. The shoe is soaked and yet

the foot remains dry. Explain that one to the panel. May the record
show sometimes there is rain and sometimes I burn butter.
Every horse is a neigh sayer. The magnets on my fridge are all very
weak. Their days numbered. Some people just want to watch
the world back burn. I stick my leg out the window of this tenancy
and sleet dampens my shinpad of a life. Better get ready for work
before I get in trouble again. I walk in the direction of work clothes,
careful not to take each day as it comes and one day posh snorkel.
The shoe is fully satched but the foot couldn't be more dry if it tried.
On my way home, a podcast to the face. I am reminded how

the first person in space was a dog. Sick of hearing it. So angry at the
sun right now I can't even look at it. What I will look at is the ibis
syphoning stormwater from potholes at the drive-thru.
My next horse will be a clothes horse. I stick my leg out the window
of this feral trickery, order a medium Quarter Pounder
Meal with a Coke. Thank you. Proceed to the next

window.

ACKNOWLEDGEMENTS

Thank you, always, to Victoria for her fathomless support. Thank you to my family and friends for continuing to enable this strange pursuit.

I am indebted to the work of Alice Becker-Ho, Fred Moten, Mark Fisher, Stefano Harney and McKenzie Wark whose conceptions of toiling under capitalism are echoed throughout.

Thank you to Kent MacCarter and Cordite Books for enlivening my words and believing in my work enough to enshrine it in a book. Also, a shout out to Egg.

Current and previous versions of poems first appeared in *The Anabranch Any Saturday, 2021, Running Westward*; *Overland*; *Cordite Poetry Review*; *Going Down Swinging*; *Groundswell: The Overland Judith Wright Poetry Prize for New and Emerging Poets 2007–2020*; *LEFT*; *Nothing to Hide: Voices of Trans and Gender Diverse Australia*; *Porridge*; *Rabbit*; *Running Dog* and a number of Red Room Poetry projects. My thanks to the editors.

'Aduantas' won the 2022 Arts Queensland Val Vallis Award. 'Cluain' won the 2022 Arts Queensland XYZ Prize for Excellence in Spoken Word. 'Creepypasta' was shortlisted for the 2021 Arts Queensland XYZ Prize for Innovation in Spoken Word and shortlisted for the 2022 Woollahra Digital Literary Award for Digital Innovation. A version of 'Everything will be okay for your landlord' was a finalist in the 2020 Queensland Poetry Festival Film + Poetry Challenge. The line 'You can run but you can't Dow Jones' is a reference to the line 'You can run / but you can't / aquarium' from 'Stingray Clapping' by Andrew Choate. 'I'M SELLING A LARGE SUITCASE?' was shortlisted for the 2020 Woollahra Digital Literary Award for Poetry. 'how_to_be_the_best_worker_in_the_world.

ppt' was runner-up in the 2021 Arts Queensland Val Vallis Award. 'A Life of Prizes' won the 2022 Harri Jones Prize as a part of the Newcastle Poetry Prize. 'No Alarms' won the Overland Judith Wright Poetry Prize in 2020. 'Old Growth / High Definition' was shortlisted for the Overland Judith Wright Poetry Prize in 2016. 'Unbelievable Meme Afterlife' was shortlisted for the 2021 Newcastle Poetry Prize. 'We're processing your direct debit' won the 2021 Woollahra Digital Literary Award for Poetry.

Dan Hogan (they/them) is a writer from San Remo, New South Wales, Australia (Awabakal and Worimi Country). They currently live and work on Gadigal and Dharug Country. In their spare time, Hogan runs the small publisher Subbed In.

www.2dan2hogan.com